GOOD YONTIF

A PICTURE BOOK OF THE JEWISH YEAR

To Sam Roth and to Sarah Roth with much love.

R.B.

To Tony, Alexandra, Julian, and my grandparents with love.

L.F.

The author thanks Rabbi Paul Kushner and Shoshana Kushner for their never-ending help and expresses heartfelt gratitude to the late Rabbi Baruch Silverstein, whose memory and spirit remain ever strong.

The artist thanks Jan Katz and Alice Nussbaum of the Jewish Education Services Department of the Jewish Community Federation of Greater Rochester, New York.

The publisher thanks Rabbi Jon Haddon of Temple Shearith Israel in Ridgefield, Connecticut.

Library of Congress Cataloging-in-Publication Data
Blue, Rose.
Good yontif : a picture book of the Jewish year / by Rose Blue;
illustrated by Lynne Feldman.
p. cm.
Summary: Information about the various Jewish holy days throughout the year follows
a series of illustrations showing a young boy and his family celebrating each holiday.
ISBN 0-7613-0142-9
1. Fasts and feasts—Judaism—Juvenile literature. 2. Fasts and feasts—Judaism—Pictorial
works. [1. Fasts and feasts—Judaism.]
I. Feldman, Lynne, ill. II. Title.
BM690.B538 1997
296.4′3—dc20 96-31054 CIP AC

Published by The Millbrook Press, Inc.
2 Old New Milford Road, Brookfield, Connecticut 06804

GOOD YONTIF
A Picture Book of the Jewish Year
by Rose Blue illustrated by Lynne Feldman

The Millbrook Press   Brookfield, Connecticut

Rosh Hashanah

Yom Kippur

Sukkot

Simhat Torah

Hanukkah

Purim

Passover

Shavuot

Shabbat

שבת

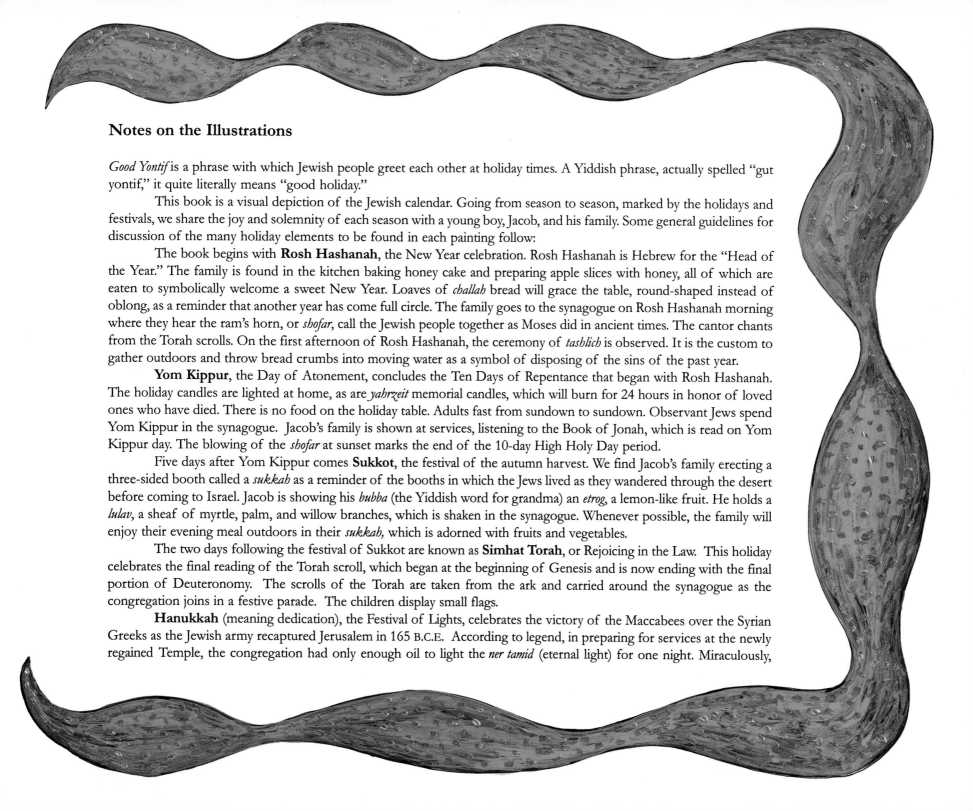

Notes on the Illustrations

Good Yontif is a phrase with which Jewish people greet each other at holiday times. A Yiddish phrase, actually spelled "gut yontif," it quite literally means "good holiday."

This book is a visual depiction of the Jewish calendar. Going from season to season, marked by the holidays and festivals, we share the joy and solemnity of each season with a young boy, Jacob, and his family. Some general guidelines for discussion of the many holiday elements to be found in each painting follow:

The book begins with **Rosh Hashanah**, the New Year celebration. Rosh Hashanah is Hebrew for the "Head of the Year." The family is found in the kitchen baking honey cake and preparing apple slices with honey, all of which are eaten to symbolically welcome a sweet New Year. Loaves of *challah* bread will grace the table, round-shaped instead of oblong, as a reminder that another year has come full circle. The family goes to the synagogue on Rosh Hashanah morning where they hear the ram's horn, or *shofar*, call the Jewish people together as Moses did in ancient times. The cantor chants from the Torah scrolls. On the first afternoon of Rosh Hashanah, the ceremony of *tashlich* is observed. It is the custom to gather outdoors and throw bread crumbs into moving water as a symbol of disposing of the sins of the past year.

Yom Kippur, the Day of Atonement, concludes the Ten Days of Repentance that began with Rosh Hashanah. The holiday candles are lighted at home, as are *yahrzeit* memorial candles, which will burn for 24 hours in honor of loved ones who have died. There is no food on the holiday table. Adults fast from sundown to sundown. Observant Jews spend Yom Kippur in the synagogue. Jacob's family is shown at services, listening to the Book of Jonah, which is read on Yom Kippur day. The blowing of the *shofar* at sunset marks the end of the 10-day High Holy Day period.

Five days after Yom Kippur comes **Sukkot**, the festival of the autumn harvest. We find Jacob's family erecting a three-sided booth called a *sukkah* as a reminder of the booths in which the Jews lived as they wandered through the desert before coming to Israel. Jacob is showing his *bubba* (the Yiddish word for grandma) an *etrog*, a lemon-like fruit. He holds a *lulav*, a sheaf of myrtle, palm, and willow branches, which is shaken in the synagogue. Whenever possible, the family will enjoy their evening meal outdoors in their *sukkah,* which is adorned with fruits and vegetables.

The two days following the festival of Sukkot are known as **Simhat Torah**, or Rejoicing in the Law. This holiday celebrates the final reading of the Torah scroll, which began at the beginning of Genesis and is now ending with the final portion of Deuteronomy. The scrolls of the Torah are taken from the ark and carried around the synagogue as the congregation joins in a festive parade. The children display small flags.

Hanukkah (meaning dedication), the Festival of Lights, celebrates the victory of the Maccabees over the Syrian Greeks as the Jewish army recaptured Jerusalem in 165 B.C.E. According to legend, in preparing for services at the newly regained Temple, the congregation had only enough oil to light the *ner tamid* (eternal light) for one night. Miraculously,

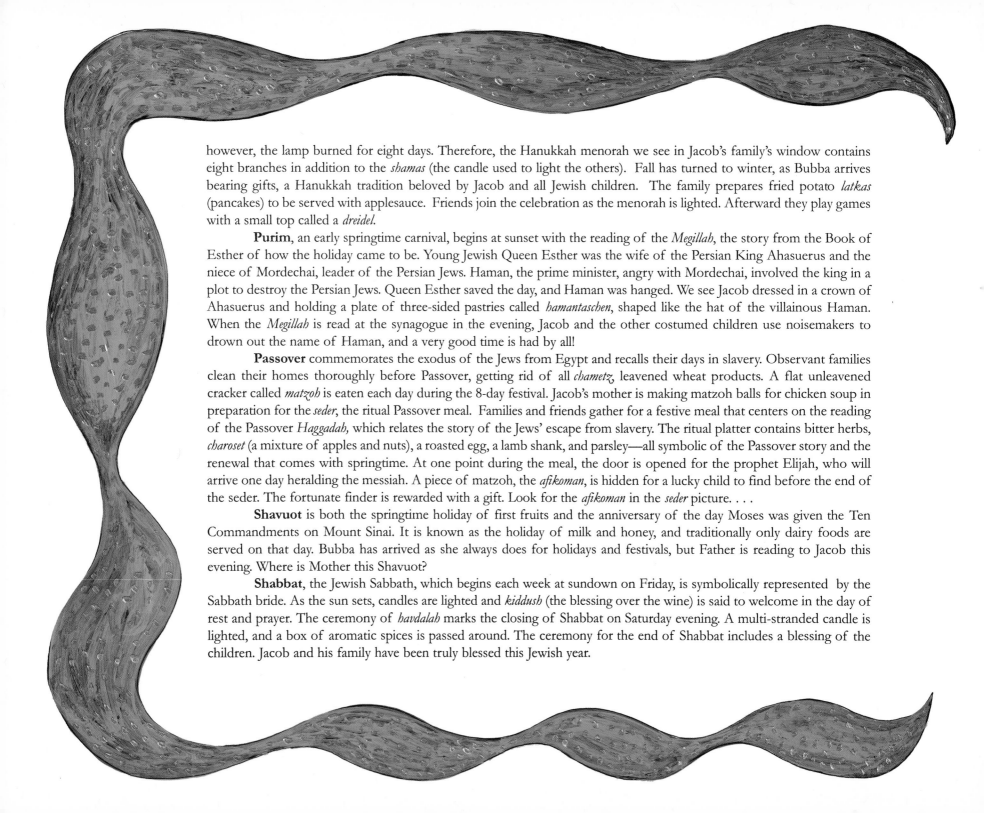

however, the lamp burned for eight days. Therefore, the Hanukkah menorah we see in Jacob's family's window contains eight branches in addition to the *shamas* (the candle used to light the others). Fall has turned to winter, as Bubba arrives bearing gifts, a Hanukkah tradition beloved by Jacob and all Jewish children. The family prepares fried potato *latkas* (pancakes) to be served with applesauce. Friends join the celebration as the menorah is lighted. Afterward they play games with a small top called a *dreidel*.

Purim, an early springtime carnival, begins at sunset with the reading of the *Megillah*, the story from the Book of Esther of how the holiday came to be. Young Jewish Queen Esther was the wife of the Persian King Ahasuerus and the niece of Mordechai, leader of the Persian Jews. Haman, the prime minister, angry with Mordechai, involved the king in a plot to destroy the Persian Jews. Queen Esther saved the day, and Haman was hanged. We see Jacob dressed in a crown of Ahasuerus and holding a plate of three-sided pastries called *hamantaschen*, shaped like the hat of the villainous Haman. When the *Megillah* is read at the synagogue in the evening, Jacob and the other costumed children use noisemakers to drown out the name of Haman, and a very good time is had by all!

Passover commemorates the exodus of the Jews from Egypt and recalls their days in slavery. Observant families clean their homes thoroughly before Passover, getting rid of all *chametz*, leavened wheat products. A flat unleavened cracker called *matzoh* is eaten each day during the 8-day festival. Jacob's mother is making matzoh balls for chicken soup in preparation for the *seder*, the ritual Passover meal. Families and friends gather for a festive meal that centers on the reading of the Passover *Haggadah,* which relates the story of the Jews' escape from slavery. The ritual platter contains bitter herbs, *charoset* (a mixture of apples and nuts), a roasted egg, a lamb shank, and parsley—all symbolic of the Passover story and the renewal that comes with springtime. At one point during the meal, the door is opened for the prophet Elijah, who will arrive one day heralding the messiah. A piece of matzoh, the *afikoman*, is hidden for a lucky child to find before the end of the seder. The fortunate finder is rewarded with a gift. Look for the *afikoman* in the *seder* picture. . . .

Shavuot is both the springtime holiday of first fruits and the anniversary of the day Moses was given the Ten Commandments on Mount Sinai. It is known as the holiday of milk and honey, and traditionally only dairy foods are served on that day. Bubba has arrived as she always does for holidays and festivals, but Father is reading to Jacob this evening. Where is Mother this Shavuot?

Shabbat, the Jewish Sabbath, which begins each week at sundown on Friday, is symbolically represented by the Sabbath bride. As the sun sets, candles are lighted and *kiddush* (the blessing over the wine) is said to welcome in the day of rest and prayer. The ceremony of *havdalah* marks the closing of Shabbat on Saturday evening. A multi-stranded candle is lighted, and a box of aromatic spices is passed around. The ceremony for the end of Shabbat includes a blessing of the children. Jacob and his family have been truly blessed this Jewish year.